THE
WHEEL
TRUTH

Don't just Survive
▪ Learn to Thrive ▪

CARLEY MEUCHEL

Design by BookCreate
www.bookcreate.com

ISBN 978-1-7923-2600-4

Printed in USA

Cover photo by
Irina Negrean Photography
www.irinanegrean.com

DEDICATION

My life has had its challenges, but through it all I've come out on the other side. I will always be grateful to my parents for giving me the wings to soar for my dreams. I dedicate this book to my family (immediate and extended) you all have supported me through the good and the bad. If I were to name you all, my heart would ache if I forgot one of you. Every one of you have guided me toward the finish line. I further dedicate this book to all my teachers and aides through school as well as my professors during college. You all took me in as a student no matter how creative you had to be. You never let my disability get in the way of my education. I started this journey knowing I wanted to be a professional speaker and the doors that have opened since then have been incredible. A SPECIAL thanks to all my mentors and coaches in the business and speaking communities. You helped me move my dreams toward reality.

TABLE OF CONTENTS

INTRODUCTION

What is
The Wheel Truth?

My name is Carley and since the minute I was born I've had to face "The Wheel Truth" even when I haven't wanted to. My life has been a book full of written, re-written, and unwritten chapters, but the one thing I've learned in the last few years is if you don't write your own chapters, others will.

Being born with a disability is often difficult because so much of your life is filled with unknowns. My parents talk about the first few years of my life being consumed with having more questions than answers. For the first few years of my life, death was a real possibility. Feeding tubes and being hooked up to oxygen were only a small part of keeping me alive. The doctors didn't care what I ate if I kept it down and it was full of fat and calories. My first two "loves" were Reese's Pieces and Coke. I was less than thirty pounds by the time I was in third grade.

As I grew older, death was less likely, but I had other challenges ahead of me. I had surgeries, more hospital stays, a combination of physical and occupational therapy which I discuss in other chapters. The questions about my life and how my disability was going to factor in became more and more complex. These questions pertained to subjects like my education, my social ability, productive employment, handling adversity, developing a certain level of independence, and so much more.

My life has progressed in such a way that most of these questions have been answered. I've had the opportunity grow my social circles. I had to stop thinking my disability was who I was because the truth is I finally understood that in order for other people not to see me as "broken" I had to stop viewing myself as "broken" and instead take "control" of my disability. When I started living for myself, rather than for everyone else, the opportunities grew stronger.

> " Believe you can and you're halfway there. "
> ~ Theodore Roosevelt

In one of my chapters of my book I talk about how I was

one of the first few to enter the public-school system and how at times it was hard because I was the pioneer for those with disabilities who followed me in education.

I was born with Cerebral Palsy. It left me unable to walk and using a power chair for mobility. This wasn't a chapter my parents, nor I thought would be, but we've made the best of it. I have had to remain positive, learn to build communities that support me, and to find joy in the small things. It has only been evident the last two, or three years how to create my life the way I want it.

Building my business as a professional speaker, I practice putting skills to work daily in every part of my life. I now hope I can take what I've learned and help you see that even if you can't control every chapter of your life, you still have control over what happens within those chapters and that's The Wheel Truth!

I'm Carley Meuchel. I'm an inspirational speaker/author equipping the disabled community to live to the best of their potential. Cerebral Palsy left me with limited lower body mobility. However, my disability hasn't stopped me from living my life to its fullest. I hope to inspire and equip others to stay positive despite the struggles in life and business; as well as teach the non-disabled community how to share success with us.

Throughout my life, I've come across people who let their circumstances define them. I've learned in the last few years, circumstances can only define me and the direction for my life if I let them. There are four things

I've implemented to create the life I have now. I learned positivity is key. Community is a must. Writing your own story is essential and finding joy is needed to make it through the tough times.

I wrote this book because I am often questioned by the disabled community about overcoming their disabilities in the real world. I, frankly, am tired of seeing people in my position struggle. I want people to know that despite a disability they still can mold the life they want and deserve.

I also want the disabled community to build a support community larger than just the people with similar challenges. Positive success began for me when I took a hold of the reins of my life and stopped waiting for something to happen. I've known for a few years now, I've wanted a business, so I went looking for multiple communities that would hold my vision alongside me. I ended up finding Toastmasters, Intuitive Speaking, Impactful People, and so many more. These are all groups who helped me not only become a better speaker and helped me grow my business, but also guided me towards a new me.

Another reason I chose to write this book is because I feel called to show the disabled community it's okay to write your own story of your life. I know for far too long I was putting limits on myself and my goals because I thought my disability and my need for federal money at the time overrode my need to feel fulfilled. The truth is once I decided to open my mind up to what could be instead of what I thought had to be I was able to create more freedom for myself. This doesn't mean the chapters within my story won't change, or that I have control over every paragraph, but my story is mine. No one else can write my story.

Lastly, I wrote this book because I need to show being positive is key. As much as I would sometimes like to, I can't wish my disability away. However, my attitude is something I can control. I stay positive by setting goals and continuing to hit milestones. I take in advice but drown out any negative talk. Positivity only grows if it's watered. I wake up every day and try and make it a good day. I don't let anyone else's attitude determine my day, or my choices. This doesn't mean I don't get down on myself however, I know if I remember these things and put them into practice daily it'll be difficult not to remain positive.

Overall, I hope my book gives audiences (specifically the disability community) the tools to live their dreams and passions at any level. No amount of money is telling me how to pursue the life I want. My community is built by people seeing me, my drive to be better and to always want more. It isn't solely built through my disability. My attitude matters in every aspect of my life. I've realized my life is what I make it and I hope my book teaches people life isn't meant to be passed by, it's meant to be lived to the fullest.

"Life doesn't just come to you. For me specifically, I knew what I wanted but didn't know how to get it. I knew I wanted independence, more income, more opportunities to meet more people and to travel.

There's a difference between knowing what you want and knowing how to go after it. I was caught in between the two. It took me a while to figure it out…but I figured it out!

I started asking, 'How?'

At the end of the day if all you're doing is only helping yourself, then that's not a really fulfilling life. I wanted to not only help myself, but to help others.

I started looking into speaking and decided I wanted to make it into a career. I explored my options. I found organizations that helped me grow toward my goals. I'm learning how to speak in front of hundreds and millions one day. Is it easy? No! But anything worth doing isn't going to be easy. I decided that sitting at home and looking out the window wasn't doing anyone any good, especially me.

I want to encourage you today whether you are disabled or not, start with small steps. Maybe that will be a painting class online and then take a studio class. Who knows where that will grow to? If I've learned anything over the last three years, it's that life doesn't just happen, you have to make it happen. You have to surround yourself with a community that supports your goals and helps you see the next step. Find the people who can help you make your dreams happen."

CHAPTER ONE

Impossible or Possible:

It's up to you!

The word disability can be scary to most if you haven't experienced it. There are so many unknowns. For my parents, this was the case. No one in my family knew what my future was going to be and because I was born weighing just two pounds, four ounces, my parents had more questions than answers. The first five years of my life was full of medical equipment, tubes, in-home care from nurses, as well as doctor visits. I also had several surgeries throughout my life.

> **If you can't fly, then run. If you can't run, then walk. If you can't walk, then crawl, but by all means, keep moving.**
>
> ~ *Martin Luther King Jr.*

When I was younger, I think I was pretty oblivious to what the word disability actually meant because I remember telling my Dad I wanted to be a firefighter when I grew up. Being the father, he is, not wanting to crush my dreams he simply said, "Ok, pal go for it."

A few years later, I realized my legs had to do something miraculous for me to pursue my future career. This was the moment where questions started popping up for me. What does disability really mean? How does it affect me?

As junior high and high school approached these questions only became more vital. I asked myself questions like: where do I fit? Where's my community? The disabled community has never really been my cup of tea, because in my opinion there's too much focus on putting everyone in the same box. It wasn't until after I was well into my college

The Wheel Truth

years, I began coming out of my shell by answering these questions on my own.

Navigating these questions, I had to figure out who Carley really was. I realized being in college for me was more than gaining some independence; it was about building my own community and learning to advocate for myself. It became less about receiving a degree and more about gaining confidence. I graduated from college with a degree in Early Childhood Education but quickly learned getting a job wasn't going to be so easy.

Having a disability whether intellectual, or physical (or both) doesn't always bode well for becoming employed, so I knew going in, I'd have issues. However, I truly wasn't prepared for just how many hurdles there would be. My father drove me around daily and helped me drop off resumes at every preschool and daycare I could find. It took a little over a month, but I received a call from a local daycare and a few days later I went in for an interview. The meeting went very well, and the director was ready to hire me on the spot. However, rarely is anything that simple.

Soon after the interview, my real troubles began. I was told by the Washington State Department of Education that I didn't have enough experience to work with children. I started to wonder what my Early Childhood Education degree was for. Then, the person who interviewed me suggested I volunteer for them so those hours could build my experience resume. I was led to believe the volunteer hours would translate into being hired. I relished the opportunity to show the daycare they had made the right decision.

Most people have good intentions, but often they don't follow through. I don't blame their motives, but at times it's their ignorance of disabled individuals' abilities that kept me handicapped. By being helpful, they failed to allow me to 'grow' into the position by doing most things for me.

Once my volunteer experience ended, I went back out driving around again with my Dad dropping off resumes. After leaving several resumes and not hearing a word from anyone I decided to enlist a little help, or what I thought was going to be help. I wasn't prepared for the adventure I was about to embark on.

Sometimes when adults with disabilities are having issues becoming employed, they ask for assistance from other agencies. This is what I decided to do. I interviewed a few different organizations first with my Dad to help me decide which one fit best for my particular needs. We then discussed it as a family and decided on one particular company. I began working with the agency several weeks later after all the paperwork was processed.

I had an in-depth "get to know you" interview called a discovery session where the agency tries to identify what you would enjoy doing for employment. I'll admit this part was difficult for me for a couple of reasons. I had spent a total of seven years in college completing an Early Childhood Education degree and had already been through the "discovery" process as part of my education. I was also raised in a family who taught us "sometimes, you just have to pick crap with the chickens" which means it's not always about what you'd love to do, but you need to get done, so you take the job that gets it done. Did I really want to work with children? No, not particularly, but continuing to build my resume was important, so I had to find something my body would allow me to do.

At our second meeting I thought if I came in prepared with my portfolio and top-notch references, I could move the meeting along. The people at the agency seemed excited, so I was encouraged, but it went down-hill from there. When asking for help from a federal governmental program, it pays to be very cautious because often-times there are strings attached. Rules and regulations of a program can sometimes prohibit an individual from reaching their full potential and this was my experience. I struggled with advocating for myself because the agency had to be involved in every aspect of the employment process even if I could handle it alone.

Are you letting society put you in a box?

Have you ever questioned your ability to do something based upon your age, gender, race, or disability? If so, do you know you're letting society put you in an invisible box? I think sometimes we have these questions and we assume we shouldn't, or we can't. The truth is we can do anything we put our minds to and are willing to work hard towards. My journey unknowingly put me in a box as well.

Having a disability gives us as well as others, the opportunity to be put in a box that some people feel is appropriate. One of the boxes, I constantly get put into is the "you have a disability so your life must be horrible" box. I've had complete strangers come up to me and ask if they can pray for me. They don't even ask me for my name, they just start praying. This drives me insane because my life is SO far from horrible, but people don't take the time to find that out. Do they give themselves a chance to get to know me? No, they just continue to make false assumptions.

There have been times where building my business has caused me to put myself in my own box. This can be dangerous because I have dreams and goals just like everyone else. I want to feel financial freedom, own my own home, and hopefully raise a family one day, and so much more. Knowing this, I've learned not to question my abilities in order to avoid the box. Boxing yourself in cheats you and gives society permission to prove society's point.

By now, you probably have a couple questions. For instance, what do I do to stay out of the box? What if I'm in the box already, how do I get out? I've come to realize staying out of the box and finding your way out of the box are the first important steps in advocating for yourself. The value of this lesson is immeasurable. What you want and need are important. Advocating for yourself can be hard, but it needs to be done. Unfortunately, I didn't learn this until well into my college years. It's also important to remember that finding out what your goals and interests are become vital to others NOT putting you in a box. Once you find those two things, you need to find a community that supports what you desire for your life. Lastly, you must know that pleasing everyone in your life is impossible and the decisions you make are exactly that, YOUR decisions no one else's.

"Ask yourself these three questions:

- What do you want?
- How can I build my community?
- What can I do to enjoy the journey?

What do you want? Do you want another job, another house, a promotion or a better circle of friends? It could be anything.

Focus on building the people and the community that you surround yourself with.

Your goals and what you want out of life, won't come flying through your bedroom window, you have to go get life.

Success means surrounding yourself with people that will help you reach your goals. Surround yourself with friends that will give you input. Find new groups of friends that will feed you with information that will propel you forward. I've found that if I surround myself with people that will help me get there, I'm not just sitting back and waiting for someone to hand me a golden ticket. It doesn't work that way.

Enjoy the journey!

Despite your ups and downs you might have, your journey has a lesson in the beginning, the middle and the end. You have multiple quests and lessons. Embrace them.

If you need someone to be in your corner, call me... enjoy the lesson and pass it forward to others with dreams."

CHAPTER TWO

Advocate for Yourself

Life often presents opportunities for us to learn from the mistakes we make. Imagine being given a situation where everyone from your family to the federal government feels they need to protect you. How are we supposed to answer our own questions, come up with our own ideas, or correct our mistakes if we aren't given the chance to experience success and failures? This was me. Everyone in my life whether I wanted them to be, or not (federal government) put me inside this invisible bubble just waiting for it to pop.

Because I was born with a disability, everyone often assumed I couldn't handle myself. This became evident when now as an adult I'm being told of situations which were handled without my knowledge. For example, until two years after I graduated from high school, I didn't know that the teacher I was supposed to have in third grade didn't want me, so I was transferred into the other classroom. The other teacher I ended up with didn't really want me either. My disability was too much of a distraction to her, but by then the school was out of third grade teachers.

> " Disability doesn't make you exceptional but questioning what you think you know about it does. "
> ~ Stella Young

In junior high, I had an instance happen where I was being kept in the dark in order to protect me. I don't know all the details of this situation, but one day I was on my way to English class when my school aide stopped to talk to one of my friend's. I overheard the aide say, "I know you were trying to come to Carley's defense, but we'll take care of it." Whatever was going to "happen" to me never did because it was being taken care of behind the scenes.

There were many times in high school where I tried to advocate for myself, but because I wasn't ever given the chance to before this, the whole concept was foreign to me. I remember when I tried to get my friends (Spencer's Own-a cappella group) to come and do a couple concerts at my school to raise money for the choir program. I went and talked to our principal and he was excited about it and he gave me the go ahead to start the process of making these concerts happen. I told him the school wouldn't have to pay a dime. After several months of phone calls, e-mails, and more with the group and their promotor, my principal canceled the concerts two days before they were to arrive. I tried to change his mind and convince him but couldn't. I believe, he thought I was incapable of pulling it off, so when he saw the date arriving, he got nervous and canceled to save me.

I often think if I would've been able to advocate for myself in these situations earlier in life it wouldn't have been so difficult for me later. The irony in all of this is I was often told I must advocate for myself by my teachers and other adults I interacted with and wondered if they realize what they're saying? How am I supposed to stand up for what I need and want when others believe I'm so fragile?

Heading into college was a different story. I was no longer in a bubble. I wasn't being kept in the dark. I knew everything that was going on. I had to build my own community by connecting with others in my classes. If I had a problem with someone, I knew about it and I found people that would help defend me if I needed defending. I found strength in knowing if I needed help, I'd have it, but I'd need to ask for it.

When it came time to find employment, it took several months. Needing "help" from a federal program placed me right back inside the bubble. I thought hiring a job coach was a good thing until rules and regulations left me unable to decide for myself and to advocate for my own needs. I knew to make a good impression, it would have been better sometimes had I gone to my interview alone, but my job coach wasn't allowed to do that. I didn't find my way out of the bubble until one of my college friends hired me at her preschool.

The opportunity to be outside of the bubble again wasn't taken lightly. For approximately the first year I felt I had to prove to my boss and friend that I deserved this chance. When there was something, I physically couldn't do I had to be honest about it. Once I had a handle on the routine, I started looking around to see what needed to be done. I knew that if I was pro-active and showed her, I could take the lead on handling discipline with the children and doing activities with them I'd be demonstrating I could do what was asked of me. I also had to be able to do enough, to avoid another person picking up the slack just for me.

Looking back on my career as a preschool teacher, I was

able to advocate for myself all the time. I didn't feel like I was in the way. My voice mattered. I wasn't seen as fragile, or someone who had to be taken care of. This was only the second time I felt allowed to explore what I was capable of.

Advocacy is a word that scared me in the beginning because I didn't learn how to do it until I was an adult. I also think my version of advocacy is different than a lot of my friends in the disabled world because it includes a different mind-set. I don't believe in demanding people do or give me something for nothing. I don't think other people should do my work for me. For instance, adults with disabilities often have the thought, "I deserve to be employed because I have a disability." I advocate for the complete opposite which is, everyone with a disability deserves the chance to try and be able to work. We can't expect employers to just give us something for nothing or create work for us to do. Productivity comes in many forms such as volunteering, entrepreneurship, community activities, and so much more.

Being your own advocate can be very intimidating if you've never done it before. For me, it was scary. For so long, I had other very well-meaning people telling me what was best for me or feeling like they had to be in "protective" mode and kept me in the dark about certain things. There are at least five things I try to remember when advocating for myself.

The first step is to remember no one knows you better than you. It's ok to get opinions and advice from others you trust. In fact, I encourage it, however, make sure those opinions and little pearls of wisdom match your needs, goals and desires.

Secondly, make a plan. It's important to have a plan because it keeps you motivated and on task; always striving for more.

Thirdly, be prepared for change. Change is inevitable. It happens. I didn't expect to spend seven years in college, or spend so much time finding employment, but I did, so I had to adjust my plan accordingly.

Fourth, be careful who you choose to be in your community. The people you surround yourself with are important. Surround yourself with a community that supports who you are to the core, your needs, and goals because you will lean on your community when times are hard. Lastly, be you, there is no one better than you—remember that!

John Furniss Speaks

"I am 100% blind, but I do not view it as a disability, more like an inconvenience. I am still able to do pretty much everything I want to do; I just have to do it in a different way than sighted folks.

I have faced many challenges in my life, and I have found that being persistent is what has helped me keep a positive attitude. It almost always pays off in the end if you are persistent. For instance, when I lose things, especially tools in my woodshop, I just have to keep looking until I find them. Generally, I am comfortable using power tools in my woodshop, but sometimes there are cuts, so I don't feel safe with a power tool. Instead, I get out my handsaw and use some old-fashioned elbow grease. I once spent all day cutting one piece of wood with a handsaw to get ready to use. Talk about persistence!"

CHAPTER THREE

Hand out
or Hand up?

*Employment
and Disability Programs*

According to Rodger W. Hancock nothing is free. He stated, "Nothing is ever free, though to you it be, somewhere, somehow, someone paid."

Growing up, my siblings and I saw our grandparents, parents, and so many other family members and friends practice a work ethic that went far and beyond the call of duty. We were taught if you can, you work for every penny earned. As adults, my brother, sister, and I have taken this to heart. My brother is an inspector for the city. My sister is a fifth-grade teacher and I'm a professional speaker. While none of our journeys to employment were smooth sailing, mine is the most challenging.

After attending college for several years, I received my degree in Early Childhood Education. I began looking for employment around Clark County dropping off resumes at every preschool available. After about a month, I was called in for an interview. Later, I discovered the Washington State Board of Education believed my two-year degree wasn't enough experience for me to work in the classroom. The director of the daycare hired me on a volunteer basis hoping those volunteer hours could eventually turn into experience hours, so she could hire me. I quickly learned the daycare wouldn't let me do anything.

After talking with my family, I decided to try a state program that helps adults with disabilities find employers willing to take a chance on us and our skill sets, and potentially hire us for a position. I took my education portfolio with me including several references, thinking this would speed up the process. I was wrong. When a state program receives federal money, they must follow certain rules. Many of these rules I feel don't encourage an employer to want to hire someone with a disability. For instance, on the few occasions where employers did call me back for an interview my employment coach would have to go with me. For me, this was uncomfortable because it didn't give me the chance to show employers that I was confident and capable. Most of the time my job coach was ready to jump in and "defend" me, or be quick to discuss accommodations, and even job carving. Job carving means an employer might have to "create" a position for someone with a disability. It costs the employer more money to hire someone who needs a position created for them than it does for the employer to hire someone who can already do the job.

> If you don't like something, change it. If you can't change it, change your attitude.
>
> ~ *Maya Angelou*

What can we do to solve this issue? In my opinion, we have two options. We can look at our skill set and see if we can help employers out with what they already need done, or we look at our own individual talents and we dive into the land of entrepreneurship. There may be options to attend trade schools. This would also encourage employers to at least give us a chance. At the end of the day, individuals with disabilities must be given the chance to try while employers need the option to say "no". We, as a community can't just demand because demanding something helps no one. We must all take a step back, look at our options and become a community that encourages hand-ups instead of hand-outs.

According to the U.S. Census Bureau people with disabilities are two times as likely to become financially stable as the non-disabled population. Is starting a business easy? No, but I had to decide if I wanted a hand-up (a community of people that I create who's willing to help me, but only if I help myself) or a hand-out (a community that throws meaningless "help" around (money) and invests in programs that produce little fruit (results). The decision is yours. Here are a few stories of individuals with disabilities who dove into entrepreneurship head-first.

Highgroundnews.com Search for entrepreneurs with disabilities.

A Parent's Thoughts ~

"My son, Kristopher was born three months prematurely 35 years ago. He was diagnosed with Cerebral Palsy at the age of six months. Those days were very different than they are today. Only in the sense that today there are endless opportunities and services available to families. That was not the experience our family had. during most of Kris's early years.

Due to the fact that Kris had a very high IQ, he was not eligible for any financial or emotional support. It was all up to my husband and I to navigate this new life we had with Kris, his twin sister and their soon to arrive, younger sister.

It wasn't an easy journey by any means. The surgeries, plus extensive appointments for physical therapy, and yearly fights with the school district, were not anything we had in common with other friends or families. It was isolating and scary. It was though, and still is, the most rewarding and joyful life I could have ever imagined. We had tremendous amounts of humor, love, and fun despite the challenges. I loved every part of my life and being Kris's mom. I wouldn't change a minute."

~Michelle Haines

CHAPTER FOUR

The Good, the Bad and the Ugly of Government Housing

What's your definition of help? Is it a hand-up, or hand-out? Do you expect something in return? These are some of the questions I consider when thinking about accepting help. However, being part of the disabled community, you don't always get to choose the kind of "help" you receive. For me, I prefer to ask for help from my growing community and exhaust all other options before involving the federal government. Many times, my disability excludes me from making my own choices.

No matter what our circumstances are almost all of us need and use the federal government for something. Sometimes the federal government has some good attached to it, but often people in society abuse the system so much it's hard to see the good. For instance, the disabled community can either take advantage of the system and all it has to offer, or other people in non-disabled (such as homeless individuals or drug addicted) circumstances take advantage of it and leave those of us in the disabled community behind. Some of the services the government tries to cover for restricted individuals as well as other groups of people are housing, employment, healthcare, and more.

> " People won't have time for you if you are always angry or complaining. "
> ~ Stephen Hawking

There are many areas where disabled adults like me try and gain more independence. One of those areas is housing. Whether you're disabled or not, everyone wants their own space. Your own space allows for unlimited privacy and a come and go policy. Many questions must be considered in order for a person with challenges to find a place to call home. These questions pertain to subjects such as affordability, amount of help the disabled person wants and needs, proximity to other places, accessibility, transportation, and more.

While there are options for disabled adults to search for housing it's extremely hard to find a house suitable for you under government rules and regulations. Occasionally agencies will host local conferences that focus on specific topics. Since I'd like to live in and own my own house one day, I thought it would be wise to attend a housing conference. During this conference, I attended a session in which all the apartments being discussed were either owned, or managed by Vancouver Housing Authority, Columbia Non-Profit Housing, and Vancouver Affordable Housing. To my knowledge, out of the thirty-eight apartments that were mentioned only two of them are for adults with disabilities and of those two sets of apartments one of them, the disabled person would have to pay rent all on their own. The other set of apartments for the disabled are only available through referral by Department of Social and Health Services (DSHS.)

Many times, people with disabilities get put in a "box." The truth is the topic of disability is more complex than a box will allow. We all have different needs and different desires when it comes to any situation in life. There are many tentacles when referring to disability, so it's difficult to come up with one cookie-cutter solution for everyone because there isn't just one. It all depends on the situation and sometimes all the rules and regulations from the government often are created for the community as a whole and doesn't allow room for looking at the individuality of a person instead.

Trying to sustain myself financially has proven to be difficult because it's almost never easy to find employment, let alone for someone with a disability. So much more needs to be included when considering the affordability of a home for an adult with a disability.

For Example:

- How accessible does your house need to be?
- How much help does the person with the disability need?
- Is the disability physical, intellectual, or both?
- Can the individual live independently most of the time, or does he or she need more care?
- How much income is being accumulated?
- Should roommates enter the equation?

All these questions and more determine affordability. Affordability goes beyond the cost of the home.

Assisted Living Facilities

Even though, they are limited but there are a few housing options for the disabled. For those aged sixty and above there are the options of senior living or assisted living. The staff at these places try and make their residents

time as pleasant as possible. Age appropriate activities
are provided at some centers such as the game bingo,
dancing, exercise classes, book clubs, and swimming to
name a few. Assisted living facilities can become expensive
when all seniors have is social security, or a retirement
check. Another person within the family may have to cover
the cost for the person living there. According to Senior
Advice on https://www.senioradvice.com/assisted-living/
vancouver-wa the cost of living in assisted living facilities
in Washington is about one-hundred and forty-two dollars
with the dollar amount needed daily being anywhere
from thirty-three dollars to three-hundred dollars. When
considering monthly prices; it ranges between one-thousand
dollars to nine-thousand dollars a month and yearly costs
being fifty-one thousand dollars.

For a young adult with a disability, an assisted living
place may not be the best idea. While it's good to be around
people who are older and wiser, it may be difficult for a young
adult with a disability to reside in assisted living. The age
discrepancy would be hard because finding things in common
with one another would be few and far between. There are
still times, however where us young adults learn a lesson,
or two from the elderly. Assisted living places who cater to
the disabled population usually have only one population
(the disabled) and while it's good to be around people who
experience some of the same struggles it's unhealthy to not
have experiences outside our disabilities and let the able-
bodied population learn from us as well as us learn from them.

Home Care

When people with disabilities want more privacy and freedom from rules and regulations homecare might be a possibility. This option also allows for more one-on-one attention where the exact needs of the disabled person are met. There are a couple down-sides if this process isn't done correctly, however. Neglect and abuse can happen. Therefore, the interview process is so vital. My family and I are doing this right now because my parents are getting older and can't physically help me as they once did, so they're moving out of the family home and down-sizing. As of now, we're in the process of finding a part-time care provider. When finding a roommate, or care provider it's important to ask about healthy relationships, family, personal goals, and moral values. An interview doesn't always provide an all-clear for neglect, or abuse, but it gives a place to begin. According to www.GeorgetownHomeCare. com under home health care costs, the national average for home care is approximately $32,760. Sometimes Medicare and Medicaid will cover the costs if the disabled person is eligible. Another element in which cost is determined is the level of care needed.

Garage Convert

Another option for housing for the disabled is a garage convert. This type of living situation works if the disabled person needs help, but only at times. He or she can have their own cozy living space and still connect with family and others when they want to or need to. This kind of situation can also become an asset when parents or legal guardians die because another responsible adult can move into the family home and be on-call if help is needed. The cost of this renovation is between ten-thousand and fifteen-thousand dollars depending on how much work is done and whether plumbing is included. This is according to www.angieslist.com and search garage conversions

Tiny Homes

One last option for the disabled would be some tiny houses. There are some concerns, however with them. They're extremely expensive. Before my parents decided on building their new house, they investigated what it was going to cost, and it was going to be ninety-thousand dollars and that's just the house. If a person must buy the land to put the house on it's even more of an investment. A tiny house does provide the opportunity for greater independence for the disabled if they have people they can call upon for assistance.

Are there housing choices for disabled people? Yes, but here's the problem. These choices are either too spendy or they're not made by us, the disabled. The choices are made by other people in our lives, or government rules and regulations which vary on a state by state basis. The truth is we're a very smart community as a whole and we can make healthy housing decisions, but we need to be given the power to make those decisions along with the choices.

Kerry Scribner Speaks~

I was born with a Central Processing Disorder, which affects the central nervous system's ability to comprehend auditory information. The CPD (Central Processing Disorder) makes it very difficult for me to understand abstract thinking or auditory information. This also affects my ability to speak and communicate with people. My mother used to describe this as "Swiss cheese" as there are many holes in the processing center of my brain.

• Communicating with people is a struggle as I have issues with understanding what someone may want me to do or explain to them.

• Simple things like "describe your favorite movie and what it's about" are like asking me to sort a pile of rocks from smallest to largest; it would take forever and after a while the listener would likely walk out on me.

• When I was young, I had difficulty talking to people and asking simple questions. For example; when I was very young, I was at a Target and I wanted to put a scoop of ice cream on a sugar cone and wanted to know how much it would cost to add sprinkles. A simple request, right? No! I asked the clerk "how much more would it be to add sprinkles?" I got the puzzled look, which, to me felt like someone was asking "what's wrong with you?" I get this a lot even in my adult hood.

I work for a communications company (can you believe that?!), I belong to a church and I frequently visit a local "Drink 'n Draw" as I am an artist. I live with my mother and have many acquaintances, whom I talk to on numerous occasions.

- At work I have LOTS of support from my peers and leadership. They rarely question my speech or communication techniques. There are times that I use a different word choice or expression that might be confusing, but I have to think fast in my line of work. That can sometimes cause auditory delay or comprehension. I must admit I am a bit hard on myself because I want to be like everyone else and not worry about what I say or "does it make sense." I tend to question myself or put myself down a lot when someone doesn't get a simple answer.

- As for my church they are so kind, and I rarely find myself in the position where I blame myself for poor word choice. I believe God gave me this "gift" to teach others to accept differences and change their communication to interact with others. Same thing with my friends. Sometimes they notice my difference when I say the wrong thing, or they have to think about what I said or what I'm asking but they can barely tell. This came from a lot of practice with my mother; rehearsing what to say and even writing it down. I was lucky that she was a special education teacher and had to learn about disabilities and how to work with kids like me.

- Drink 'n Draw is my "Justice League" or people

who understand that I might be different but they don't have me there to purely talk in words. I get to use my true form of communication: drawing. I'm a visual person and that's how I have been able to "talk" to others.

When I was a kid I would draw everything; comic book strips, illustrations of what I saw, how I felt, lots of fictional characters, animals, flowers, etc. My mother took me to a therapist's office when I was very young (5 or 6) and, while we were waiting to be seen I started to draw my mother's paisley dress. The dress had many details, which I picked up in my drawing. I finished the piece during the conversation my mother had with the physician as the conversation wasn't as appealing as my graphite on recycled paper. The therapist stopped for a moment and asked to see the piece. He was so impressed that he asked to keep the picture, claiming that I would grow to be a famous artist due to my audio impairment and my ability to communicate through pictures. I drew quite often as a child and found joy in illustration. One of my dreams is to become a professional comic book artist.

I stay positive by reciting this: "It's not always you, Kerry. It's them." Giving recognition for things I do well and learning from my mistakes keeps me positive. It's not always easy as I try to dismiss the fact that I have a different learning style. I had to learn that I can't ignore the fact but it's not bad having this challenge in my life.

Other people need to learn to work with me and allow me to be myself. I'm not dumb; in fact I'm quite smart!

I love to read articles, non-fiction books and watch movies; especially documentaries and independent films (art house, film festival movies, etc.) I'm an artist so I enjoy drawing and learning about art history. I go to comic book shows and art events. I attend a Drink 'n Draw on Wednesday nights and life drawing classes when I can. I'm also attending private lessons from a comic book artist to further my skills as an illustrator. For 5+ years now I've attended the Clark County Fair and even demonstrated my artistic skills in public. This proved that I don't need to speak to communicate for people to understand me.

For years I've wanted to give up my CPD for normal audio comprehension, but I've learned that It's just not in the cards. God made me this way. In fact, I think he meant for me to have CPD to be compassionate to others who may have a difference like mine or more severe. I have a great deal of respect for those who struggle with their personal demons or differences. Yes, I would love to be a "normal person" by not having to think about what I'm going to say when someone asks me "I see you read a book. What was it about?" and just answer the question. It's very painful and causes me to doubt myself when I can't answer a question that should be easy. I know what I want to say but it's like the Swiss cheese example: I have a lot of holes. There are parts missing and I can't get those parts back; there's no possible way.

The able-bodied community responds in different ways; it's all about perspective and instance. Many don't see it (I must be REALLY good at containing/masking my disability) and are shocked when I tell them about my CPD. Others don't believe it or think it's not a big deal. There are some who think I'm dumb or have an issue when I struggle to communicate like everyone else and I get teased sometimes. This is very rare in our modern age of accepting people of different learning styles.

- I am so relieved to see videos or read articles of good people who get to know people with disabilities or want to work with them. I have a good friend who enjoys talking with me and thinks I'm intelligent BECAUSE I have a difference. I feel like I could fly when I hear that I'm smart or intelligent.

- There will always be times that my CPD will get in the way but if I continue to be positive and not worry it won't be as prevalent.

My mother was a special ed teacher and my father taught regular ed students in Junior High and High School. I don't know if it was particularly stressful for my mother to raise me but the stress would most likely come from the fact that my father left my and brother and I when I was 3, my brother was 8. Dad had difficulty communicating with me and reacted unkindly. I would get in trouble a lot as a kid, causing PTSD (still deal with it as an adult) so I was thankful that my mother raised me. Sure, she would get frustrated with me but that was normal. She would defend me when she saw the "behaviors" as a cause of my difference. I couldn't process abstract thoughts or understand auditory commands/instructions like most kids.

- As for coping with my dad I was constantly reminded by my mother that it wasn't me. He didn't stick around to raise me or understand how he needed to talk to me. Even now he ignores the fact that I have CPD.

- Mom and I would rehearse proper sentences and situations where I might need to change my behavior or how to react to someone. We would write down what to say when I spoke with my dad and for years my father thought I was repeating what my mother said. The fact is I couldn't put the right words together. I was frightened and stressed whenever I had to talk to someone, especially my dad. Writing things down and coming up with common sentences to his responses allowed me to get out my thoughts and counteract the stiffness in my communication.

My mother took me to Dr. Labs when I was a young kid and in my 20's just after I dropped out of the Art Institute of Portland. I needed the testing to show that I was dealing with a difference. What we learned from these tests is I have difficulty interacting with others and processing complex subjects such as math, science and anything dealing with numbers. School has been a struggle. It wasn't until the 4th grade that I was able to read. Tough life.

- I had lots of help from my school in the special ed department when it came to reading, math and daily school life. My mother went to a therapist by the name of Ellen Arwood who taught her how to use images and draw things out; showing me how to get ready for school, how to clean my bedroom, pack a lunch, what I need to pack for a trip, etc. She would also give me a visual of what my body needs to look like when I do something (in a church, movie theatre, restaurant). These images were hand drawn stick figures, which showed me what I needed to look like in a specific situation. We would also use thought bubbles of what I might be thinking or what to say "make it sound like this." Having CPD it was hard for me to get my thoughts out in an auditory fashion so these practices were very helpful.

- As an adult I sought the assistance of the DVR, which was one of the biggest mistakes I made. I don't want to leave a bad reputation in anyone's mind when it comes to the DVR. I had a bad case worker and I'm sure there are plenty of amazing people. I got the bad apple. However, that being said I did get some amazing help from NNRI (I believe they are no longer with us), who helped me get a job and learn to use the gifts I have as a result of my difference. My disability makes it extremely difficult to narrow things down and explain things simply. NNRI helped me take the skills I DO have, and put them into a laundry list of things companies are working for. This organization specifies in helping people with differences find jobs and staying in one.

When it comes to inappropriate questions about my disability, I am much more mature than you might suspect. If someone says, "are you stupid?" I simply say, "oh no! Would I be stupid if I graduated with honors and can read a book in 1 hour?" I've written two books and I frequently visit the book-store/library. My speech was teased a bit as a kid, but my mother came up with some great ways to turn it around. I have had some struggles at work where someone might ask what is wrong with me. I think it's honestly because my peers aren't willing or don't know how to react to someone with my hidden disability. It's not as obvious as someone who has a physical disability but it's still there. I have to recite my question in my head or in the mirror before I go to work, so I catch up with other people as to not get in trouble or teased. I've worked really hard to not let my disability show.

Living with a disability is both a blessing and a curse at times. I'm saddened to think that I wanted to leave this earth because I was different or couldn't communicate like others but if you EVER feel that way just know you have people who are just like you and are always on your side. NEVER listen to someone who says, "someone has it worse than you." That is a HORRIBLE thing to say and they never had to live a moment in your shoes. You are NOT a mistake and there are good people who can help you. The trick is finding the right person. I was blessed to have my mother and amazing therapists who came up with some amazing skills, allowing me to communicate. I don't think I will ever get over my disability but I have come a long way from a kid who couldn't order an ice cream cone with extra sprinkles to a full time billing agent who has to communicate for a living and is doing quite well. I've been in customer service for 15 years with a number of awards and recognition, not to mention multiple customers who have benefited from my knowledge. It's all about working with your disability and using it as a tool rather than a crutch. You CAN do anything; the first step is coming up with a goal, figuring out what steps you need in order to reach that goal and then following through on those steps. If one school, teacher, case worker, physician, psychiatrist, etc, doesn't work out then go to someone else. And don't feel like you have to keep your feelings inside. Allow yourself to grieve. It's tough having to live with a difference but it's easy when you put tools in your way that will make those difficulties obsolete.

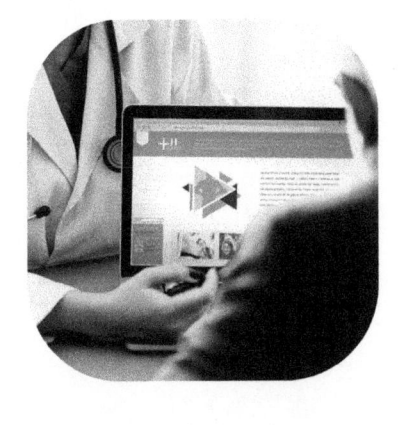

CHAPTER FIVE

The Good, the Bad and the Ugly of Healthcare

There are many views on healthcare. Is it a right, or a privilege? When people abuse the healthcare system, over and over again, should healthcare continue to be free to them? What if a person isn't abusing the healthcare system, but can't afford it? What about people who only receive Medicare and Medicaid? Since some doctors won't take either one, how do the elderly or the disabled afford their care? How does a person apply for healthcare? These are some of the questions people are debating and exploring when discussing this topic.

It's probably different for each state, but in the state of Washington, Apple Care is one of the options for free or low-cost healthcare. I have this particular healthcare coverage because I have a disability and have an income other than Social Security. I specifically receive Apple Health Care for Workers with Disabilities (H.W.D) because I'm self-employed. A person with a disability doesn't have to be self-employed to receive H.W.D., he or she must be working, and your age must be sixteen through sixty-four. This whole process is based on an income that could change month to month. The premium for HWD is based upon a portion of income. The cost will

> " My advice to other disabled people would be, concentrate on the things your disability doesn't prevent you doing well, and don't regret the things it interferes with. Don't be disabled in spirit as well as physically. "
>
> ~ *Stephen Hawking*

not rise above seven and a half percent and may be less. To find out more about Apple Health, or to see if you qualify visit: www.healthplanfinder.org

Medicare

Medicare is the federal health insurance for people of retirement age (65 and over), younger people with disabilities also can receive it, or people with end-stage renal failure. I receive both part A and B of Medicare. Some of my doctor visits get covered by Medicare as well as certain medical equipment for my disability. However, fewer medical professionals are willing to take Medicare coverage because they get paid very little for their services. My father has had to pay my entire doctor bill at times because Medicare coverage has come two to three months late. Reports have suggested Medicare will likely go bankrupt in the coming years if something isn't done. To read more on Medicare visit: https://www.medicare.gov/index

Free Health Care

When we talk about "free healthcare" let's remember it's free only to the patients, but not to the taxpayer. While, I think there are a lot of honorable people who need the availability of free healthcare there are still some people who like to take advantage of the word free. For example, what about alcoholics or drug addicts who want to keep living a dangerous lifestyle? Should we, the taxpayers pay for their bad choices? I understand this is my opinion, however this is currently happening, and we can only help those who want to be helped.

Options 360 is a clinic that helps young women with their unplanned pregnancies. It's free to the patients who come in, and it has medical professionals who care about the well-being of the young parents and their baby. This clinic provides enough stability as well as emotional support, so the young mothers and their partners can make wise, well-informed decisions throughout their pregnancies. Some of the services offered through this organization are pregnancy testing, limited ultrasound, education, and more. My family attends the banquets every year. To learn more about this organization go to: https://options360.org/

If people don't have healthcare insurance, it can cause difficulties later on down the road. As people grow older, they sometimes require more medical attention and paying for procedures, medical equipment, and doctor visits, can get expensive when it comes strictly out of your pocket. For me, my disability makes everything more expensive, so I can't afford all out of pocket expenses. I need a power chair, a manual chair, an accessible van, and so much more. The power chair I have now was almost twenty-thousand dollars by it-self. All of these things would have been impossible to obtain without insurance.

My disability allows me to be on my father's retiree insurance because I've been disabled since birth and we can use it for my supplemental insurance. Once my father passes away, we don't know what happens to it. We don't even know if my mother will be able to stay on it. The fact that my mother and I are dependents also applies to us utilizing the insurance.

My father is as healthy as a horse, so seldom does he need the insurance. On the other hand, my mother's Rheumatoid Arthritis (RA) requires a ton of medications to keep the pain, stiffness, fatigue, swelling and loss of physical ability at bay. She just started receiving injections to help with her physical function. RA attacks the heathy joints of the body and is a chronic disease that never goes away.

To learn more about RA visit: www.Humira.com/rheumatoid-arthritis

For those that don't want governmental healthcare here are some options. A person or family could always pay out of pocket if they wanted to and could afford to do so. Yes, this isn't the most economical, but it can be done.

Medishare

Medishare is also a possibility. Medishare is an organization for Christians to share their medical needs with one another. It's private healthcare where people can lift the financial burden off each other and share medical bills. It was founded in 1993 and since then, there are over four-hundred thousand participants and over 2.6 million dollars have been shared and discounted. To find out more check out: https://mychristiancare.org/medi-share/

Homeopathic Medicine

Some people look for a holistic and natural approach to being treated, cared for, and cured. This is where a homeopathic can help. A homeopathic' s job is to focus on the body as a whole as well as the person and not just the "sick" part. They stay away from conventional drugs and give the body a chance to heal itself through healthy foods like vegetables, minerals, and animals in nature. To learn more visit: https://homeopathyusa.org/homeopathic-medicine.html

Specialty Donation Hospitals

St. Jude's hospitals focuses on helping children defeat their diagnosis of cancer and other life-threatening diseases. Some of these diseases are brain cancers, blood cancers, and bone cancers. These hospitals are run almost completely on donations. This is so parents can make their sick children the first priority and not have to worry about medical bills. To donate to these brave little souls, visit: www.stjude.org

Shriners Hospitals provides care for children with neurological and skeletal disabilities. I was a patient for them in Portland, Oregon. I had some appointments there and even had a quad surgery done there as well. I also attended occupational therapy there where I practiced daily living skills. I aged out of their system once I turned eighteen. To learn more about Shriners Hospital and how they help children be sure to visit: https://lovetotherescue.org

Life with disabilities has its own unique challenges and healthcare shouldn't be one of them. Here are three ways I see improvements can be made. First, as a patient ask questions. It seems like every part of government nowadays is full of bureaucracy and in my opinion, it became that way because we don't ask questions. Second, as a patient, be clear and concise about what you want and desire. Remember, your doctor is there to help guide your decisions, so you can make the best, informed decision possible, but he or she can't make the decision for us. You know your body the best. Lastly, remember the system can be hell, but if you fight through it and don't give up you will get through it.

"Be a believer and then a doer!

Three years ago, when I started this journey of building a business and knowing I wanted to become a speaker and then an author, I had no idea how to start, who to talk to and what to do. I just knew I wanted to be an entrepreneur and knew I was clueless. I had to start by believing that I could do this. That I could set up a plan and that I could successfully execute it. My friends in the entrepreneur world shared with me that I didn't have to have it all figured out but to get started. So, I just started.

Believing isn't enough, I had to start moving.

Has it been easy? NO! It has not been easy by any means, but I figured it out. I found there is joy in the journey in just figuring out what to try next. Somethings I do right, somethings I don't, but that's part of the journey. Have I accomplished all I want to yet? No! But the joy of figuring it out has been exciting. If I could encourage you today with one thought, it's this…don't just be a believer, be a doer and enjoy the journey."

CHAPTER SIX

Are You Telling Your Story?

Stories can impact our lives in ways that are unforeseen whether it's your own story, or someone else's. I believe any story has miles of power whether it shows up right away or somewhere down the road. The only question I have for you is are you telling yours? There are many reasons a story should be told. Here are the top three reasons I've learned to tell mine.

Your Story Matters

Truthfully, I haven't always wanted to tell my story because the word "inspiration" gets tossed into the conversation almost instantly. I want to make an impact in others' lives, but not for the reasons you may think. My friends and I, in the disability community, might be labeled an "inspiration" just for breathing. Now, I do have friends that use certain tools to help them breathe, but it's just part of their story and they're grateful for those things that help them. For me, I hope I can teach and show others that story matters beyond their circumstances and it's what we do within those circumstances that makes our story matter.

> " You can't go back and change the beginning, but you can start where you are and change the ending. "
>
> ~ C. S. Lewis

Your Story Does Make an Impact

Even when we think our story won't have an impact, our

story determines the power. I remember when I was little, I was one of the few children with a disability that attended public school. Through some of my experiences, the staff, my parents, as well as myself learned there had to be some major changes. Unfortunately, some of these changes took place after I graduated from high school, but I take pride in being a pioneer and helping pave the way for future students when it comes to accessibility. This wouldn't have happened had my story not had an impact.

Make Sure You're the One Telling Your Story

I've come to realize the importance of YOU telling your story. Now, I'm NOT saying you shouldn't listen to ideas, or take suggestions from others about the direction of your story, but you're the writer, so make sure the chapters align with the story you want to be told. The chapters may change and that's ok, however always remember you're the author!

CARLEY SPEAKS

"Starting to build a business was not easy. When I thought about doing it, it took me forever to make up my mind. The more I thought about it, the more it became clear to me I have to be open to opportunities and the possibilities that my life was more than my circumstances and my life is more than a disability.

Be open to opportunities and the doors will open!

I had to be open, set goals for my life and basically become a new me with a new mindset. I thought about what I wanted. I knew I wanted to enlarge my community. I knew I wanted more people in my life that would help me be more independent by defining how I wanted to receive help. I didn't know how I was going to get it done but the process has been rewarding."

CHAPTER SEVEN

See the Light
Through the Darkness

In the past, I've been called, "the pioneer" for children and adults with disabilities. I used to hear that term but as a child I was oblivious to what that meant. Now as an adult, understanding peers need new thinking, I proudly wear it as an invisible badge of honor. Although it can be difficult at times, I leave the badge on and wear it because people deserve to know how to see the light despite the darkness, so they can create the life they desire.

I feel there are many responsibilities when it comes to embracing the role of the pioneer. One of those comes in the form of answering questions. Do I always want to answer them?

> " Optimism is the faith that leads to achievement. Nothing can be done without hope and confidence. "
>
> ~ Helen Keller

No, but it's my chance to educate children and adults that life is truly what you make it. Sometimes the questions are innocent because they often come from a child-like curiosity. For instance, a statement from a five-year-old like, "I can go to the bathroom, but you can't," gives me the opportunity to explain that I use special equipment to help me. I often get the "How come you use a power chair?" question from children as well. My response usually entails something like "Because my legs are broken and won't work like yours." I never mind these questions from innocent hearts.

If I'm being honest, however I give children far more slack with their questions because they're still learning and still developing common sense. Sometimes, adults on the other hand drive me crazy because they make assumptions of what I can and can't do. My favorite statement adults say is, "Your life must be horrible." I try hard not to crack up laughing because I don't want to embarrass them, but sometimes I find it hilarious how clueless people can be. I don't see my life as horrible at all.

Sometimes people say, "You're an inspiration." I don't mind when people that know me say that because they're putting context behind it, it's not because I'm disabled. Another question adults' often ask me is, "How do I stay so positive?" The answer is I'm not always positive, but I try to be. I can't change the fact I have a disability; however, I can change my circumstances around it.

My parents just finished building a retirement home just for them. In the meantime, they hired a young married couple to live with me until I can afford to buy a mobile home and live on my own. This has been extremely hard on me because I'm thirty-two years old and I wasn't as much a part of the hiring process as I would have liked. I also had other ideas on how to interview potential assistants and would have preferred more input in the procedure. If I'd been able to say yay, or nay and had the final say I'd feel much better.

One of the reasons I'm as positive as I am is because I've learned being miserable all the time doesn't help anyone, especially me. It doesn't help me accomplish the goals I have set for my life or help the people I love and care about rally around me to help me be the best I can be.

The Wheel Truth

When trying to start a friendship or build a community with someone with a disability ask them questions that aren't related to their disability. What are your hobbies? Do you have a job? What's your favorite food? Where do you like to go on vacation? Tell me about your family. Let us bring up our disability, because then we're in charge of the conversation. When we feel we can trust you and you're not just interested in what's wrong with us, we're then able to let you in.

In my opinion, some people with disabilities find it difficult to build a relationship (friendship or otherwise) with the able-bodied population because they feel they won't understand their disability or them, so they don't attempt to go any further. I also think the disabled community tends to believe the abled-body individuals has a "you are my enemy" mentality. I believe if we carry around this mentality all the time we could miss out on some amazing friendships and relationships. As a community, we can't assume everyone is "out to get us" because it leaves us miserable, bitter, and without a community. Personally, I've noticed my community consistently growing with the able-bodied because I've opened myself up to more. It hasn't been easy; however, I've stopped listening to the other voices that would hold me back (some of whom I love dearly) and started living the life I know I was meant to live. I know some of my relationships may think they're protecting me and don't see that in truth they are stifling me instead. I love them for it, but I had to start deciphering what was best for me.

Things began to turn around for me about three years

ago. I knew I wasn't going to teach my whole life, so I began thinking about the kind of opportunities I wanted to have available. I love to travel. I own an accessible van which gets me anywhere I need or want to go. I love meeting new people and making new connections as well as being an influence in people's lives. People have told me I'd be an excellent speaker, so I started really considering it as an actual career path and pursuing it as an option. It took a while, but once I got out of my own way, the doors blew open. It's been amazing. If the disabled community stops limiting themselves according to what other people want and what the state wants almost anything would be possible. For me, it came down to defining what I wanted, committing to it, and creating a community who would help me get there.

I think in some way or another we've all been rejected or dealt with immature, inexperienced, or ignorant people. Throughout my life, I've had to deal with several rejections and ignorance. When I was little, people assumed I couldn't hear, speak, or understand. As a family, we'd go out to eat and the server would ask my parent's, "what does she want to eat?" My father would respond, "I don't know, ask her." My favorite one has always been, "what's her name?" I remember after I came with an assistance dog from Canine Companions for Independence (CCI) strangers thought I was blind. I thought to myself, read his vest, do I look blind to you? I can only recall a couple of times during my school years where I was rejected, but I was never the popular student. I never felt real rejection until I was trying to become employed. When employers aren't honest with you about why they won't hire you, it hurts. I understand why they can't tell the truth, but it still stings. All of this is hard sometimes, but I give myself the chance to feel the emotions I'm feeling at the time and then let it go because it's not worth obsessing over.

Life does have its moments of darkness, but if we try and see the glimmer of light we're headed in the right direction. We also need to cultivate the light by bringing people around us who illuminate the light and shine so bright. It's important to share it as well.

A Parent's Thoughts ~

"One thing that really helped me was getting connected to organizations for parent support in my community and also organizations connected to my child's/children's special needs. It helped with getting information and getting support as a parent. Also, it helps to meet other parents with children with the same or a similar disability. Two of my girls have had a mentor help them navigate problems and they in turn have been able to mentor others as they are now adults themselves.

There are so many groups with websites or closed Facebook groups where your information is not broadcast across the entire planet.

You can be as active or inactive as you want."

~ Sue

Kris Haines Speaks~

My disability is Cerebral Palsy. I'm a full-time wheelchair user. My community is the local theatre community. I assume I first attract their attention in crowds because of the chair, but I like to think that they stay interested due to what I have to say. Also, my website of reviews gained all of its press-credentials from a speech I made to the city council in support of a wheelchair friendly theatre. This taught me there is great benefit to be found in facing one's fears. I hadn't done much public-speaking since late-childhood.

I've learned to stay positive in my circumstances almost exclusively by getting out and doing things. Nothing lets depression take over more than simple boredom and isolation.

I invest in my hobbies: writing, theatre, concerts, movies, audiobooks/books and anything that interest me.

I focus on staying positive. I don't think there is anything inherently positive about a disability. The most depressing thing for me is the missing of the typical milestones of independence: 1st car, 1st job,

1st apartment. That said, I continually force myself to remember that able-bodied people struggle to maintain those things, and I do not. Also, I find it a relief to be a passenger. Driving really seems scary/nerve-wracking from the backseat.

I don't find that the able-bodied community responds intentionally negatively to my disability. In fact, throughout my entire childhood I can think of only one incident in Kindergarten, when a much older (fifth-grader) made an insulting comment about my impaired drawing ability. He didn't even intend to be mean and later apologized. That's pretty good, I've heard bullying horror stories from others. In fact, the worst, truly hurtful comment I ever heard was said by a person I would've hoped should've known better. It was my very first attempt to look for employment. This job-developer came to my home, and as she learned that my ambitions far-exceeded those of most of her clients, she flat-out told me she was at a loss about how to proceed. That wasn't the insult, I appreciated her honesty. Later, I ran into her at her workplace, and she admitted when she first met me she, "did not match my mind to my body." I knew what she meant, but it has echoed in my head for years, because I have a deep fear that many able-bodied people "write me off" due to the obviousness of my physical disability.

The Wheel Truth

CHAPTER EIGHT

The Secret Sauce
to the Teacher-Student
Relationship

According to Albert Einstein, "Education is not the learning of facts, but the training of the mind to think." A good education has always been a staple in our family since both sides of my family, as well as my immediate family, are all teachers. I learned quickly to hold education in high regard, but I also found out having a disability and having challenges were not going to escape the educational system.

There were so many elements my parents, and I had to think about and questions we had that to this day we still don't have answers to, however, there was always one crucial piece it took time to build and it was relationships. My parents and I had to create a bond with the entire staff really, but especially with my teachers. School relationships were sometimes challenging but always necessary for a productive school year.

> " Hard things are put in our way, not to stop us, but to call out our courage and strength. "
> ~ Unknown

In my early years of school, I had some fantastic teachers. I was treated with dignity and respect by many of them. Most never acted as if my disability was a hindrance to my education. There were many good school year memories. My second-grade teacher would always test me on my times' tables on the way out to my bus at the end of the day. One year I came down with a horrible case of pneumonia, and he and his family came to visit me in the hospital.

In fourth grade, I had to have major surgery on my

stomach. I can't remember how many days I missed of school, but while I was in the hospital, my teacher had my classmates write get-well cards to let me know they were thinking of me. I felt so special. My aide from school came to see me, and we looked through them together.

When I entered fifth grade, I had the opportunity to attend outdoor school with the rest of the fifth graders. Outdoor school was a big deal for me because my disability can sometimes prevent me from participating in specific trips or activities if I don't have enough physical help available. All the adults who were going with us agreed to rally around me when I needed assistance. I still couldn't do everything the other students did; however, being there was enough to make me feel like I was part of the experience. I was awarded the "courage" wooden necklace at the end of the week.

While most of my early years in school were remarkable, my third year was the "test." There were two teachers who taught third grade at the elementary school. The teacher I was supposed to have didn't want me because I would have been too much of a "distraction." I was put into the other teacher's classroom; however, my disability was also a burden to her. My walker made too much noise, and by using my walker, it made me late to class. She didn't appreciate that at all. I was also taken out of class for physical and speech therapy twice a week. The teacher became irritated at this as well.

Junior high and high school were in classes of their own. There were highs and lows. Most of my teachers in these last years were fantastic. I remember my math teacher in junior high was also the basketball coach, and she knew I loved basketball, so she let me run the scoreboard for all the home games. I was so happy to be "part of the team."

My high school years were more of the same. I had some excellent teachers. I remember what one of the teachers I had, when I was a senior, said to me, "the only reason I'm going to graduation is because of you and another student." I not only was happy he was attending graduation, but I respected him as a teacher so much. I also liked my Spanish teacher because I could go into his classroom before school even began and get homework help from the night before and boy did, I need it. He also related to his students quite well.

There were some hard times during high school. I remember asking the basketball coach if there was something, I could do to help the team. He said he would think about it and get back to me. He never did. There was another incident that happened with the high school principal that I share about in another chapter.

Overall, I think my years in school were pretty good. If I could impart some wisdom to other students (especially those with disabilities) it would be three things:

- Know who you are as a student. Set your own goals for the year. I sometimes made the mistake of not knowing what I wanted, or at least not using my voice strongly enough, so I could be heard. Therefore, my teachers had a personal agenda for my education.

- Be as open and honest as you can. Disabilities are

The Wheel Truth

tricky, and if your teacher hasn't been around them, they won't always know what to do or say; have some grace, be patient with them, and let them ask questions. However, don't let your disability become an excuse not to do what's required.

It's essential to have the right attitude. My teachers almost always knew that I had to work "extra" hard and long hours as well as being excluded from some physical activities, but because I never took my anger and frustration out on them, they were almost always in my corner cheering me on.

I finally got smart and hired a coach. I reached out to those who can move me along my dreams. I've met fantastic people who have helped me. My smart move was to find people who could coach me to my best advantage and bring out my strengths. Are there bumps in the road? Yes, but I know I can get through them.

This is a marathon, not a sprint, but I'm running the race.

The truth is I just had to get started. There are so many people willing to help, but I had to say, "I need help." I've built a friendship tribe and a business tribe and am living a life without regrets and on the path to realizing my goals and dreams.

CHAPTER NINE

The Battle Over the Driver's Seat:

Are you in charge or is someone else?

Being born with a disability has its on-going struggles. Some struggles can be physically seen while others are easily hidden. The ones that are harder to see are the emotional times where you sometimes have to be your own cheerleader. Don't get me wrong, I'm not saying your family and friends won't support your dreams or goals if you have a disability, however sometimes their versions of our futures aren't ours. This can be a struggle for us all even if you don't deal with a disability.

Whether you have a disability or not, we sometimes have people in our lives who try and mold us into who they want us to be as well as what they want us to do. They often think they are showing love and protecting us. For me, my disability allows people (who I know love me) as well as people who don't know me (the state) to dictate their vision for my life. This makes it difficult for me to be in the driver's seat.

I have found ways to deal with this challenge though. I remind myself that even when there may be doubt in others' minds, there can't be doubt in mine. I have to believe the future I want and work so hard to get is possible. The other aspect I have to remember is I can't control others' emotions or thoughts around what my plans are. People have a right to their feelings no matter what they are. It's my responsibility to listen with respect even if I think or know what is right for me.

At the end of the day, it's our life and while many of us are put in the passenger's seat for different reasons we need to figure out how to be in the driver's seat one hundred percent of the time or as often as possible. This doesn't mean we don't accept change, advice or resources, but we decide if and when. No one else can or should make it for us. For instance, I couldn't control my diagnosis of Cerebral Palsy (CP), however I can control my life with it in mind. We all have certain diagnosis or traumas we face in our lives; we can run from them or face them head-on and STILL remain in the driver's seat.

Sometimes being in control can be scary, but that's when you call on the community of people you trust to keep you grounded and help you reach your fullest potential. Three years ago, when I began the journey of becoming a speaker, author, and all around change-maker I knew I needed to surround myself with mentors, coaches, as well as others who wouldn't try and change my path or re-write my story, but help me stay in the driver's seat, so I can help others do the same.

> **❝ If you always put limit on everything you do, physical or anything else, it will spread into your work and into your life. There are no limits. There are only plateaus, and you must not stay there, you must go beyond them. ❞**
>
> *~ Bruce Lee*

What does staying in control look like? Here are ten ways to help you take control of your life and keep it:

- When trying to help someone with a disability it's important to assess the situation. Does he or she need help and if so with what and how much? The "caretaker" or a friend will have to ask some questions in order to determine the level of help that's needed.

- Some people with disabilities are open books and some choose not to be, so you may need to include others in their support system to volunteer some information at times. Currently, a husband and wife team has moved in with me to assist me with certain personal needs like bathing, driving, and occasionally other activities as well.

- It's also important to have accessible living spaces for those with physical disabilities. My father made my bathroom totally accessible complete with a grab bar as well as a roll-in shower.

- Whether you were born with a disability or became disabled later in life it can be difficult to accept limitations. We need to learn we'll have highs and lows like everyone else does. What's crucial is not obsessing over what we can't change, but instead focusing on what is possible.

- When it comes to your disability, you're your best advocate. You know what you need and desire, so ask for help when it's needed.

- In order to take control of your life you first have to decide what it looks like for you. What can

The Wheel Truth

you personally gain from taking control? For me, it's so many factors. My main concerns are my independence as well as life-changing decision making. Right now, I'm still in the position where not everything is up to me, but I'm confident with time the bubble wrap will come off and people will begin to accept the decisions I make for myself.

- It's sometimes easier for the disabled community to let others' "take control". I think it's because we're afraid of disappointing our loved ones along with not following the "rules" and "regulations" (the state). These two factors sometimes contradict what a person with a disability truly needs and desires. However, in the words of Joseph Campbell who says, "If you see your path laid out in front of you step by step, you know it's not your path. Your own path you'll make with every step you take. That's why it's your path." I want you all to reflect on that quote and remember it's not the steps of everyone else that makes your life, it's the steps YOU personally take. If you choose to let life just pass you by, guess what? It will.

- If you can't do multiple tasks a day to get closer to your goals and desires, do at least one a day. This often brings a sense of accomplishment to your soul and will put a smile on your face. For me, as long as I do, I'm content.

- Remember to always give yourself grace. None of us

are perfect. We all make mistakes disability or not. Always keep trying and ALWAYS remember who's in charge.

- Always be building your community. Get to know a wide variety of people. You can't be everything, or know everything, so having a deep well of contacts increases your own opportunities. As a speaker and author, I've had many occasions to get out in the community and build relationships of all kinds which builds my opportunities.

Life is truly like a car. It can change directions in the blink of an eye. Remember when it happens, you still have control and you can still take the lead, but you may have to re-route. It's important to always keep your eyes and ears open while listening to your heart to find out where to drive next.

"In society, as a general rule, we may struggle with three questions. Who am I? Where do I belong? What are my values? For me, the hardest question growing up was where do I belong? On one hand, finding my community as a child was pretty easy because in a way it was built in. I automatically became part of the disability community the minute I was born. As a child being part of a like-community was a saving grace because I knew that no matter what I was going through there was someone going through the same thing. However, I've found it harder to be part of the disability community as an adult because our needs, wants, as well as our overall direction for our lives change.

As a child in school, I had classmates I completed projects with and played with at recess, so my community was there. However, once junior high and high school rolled around it was much harder. My classmates were involved in sports and other activities. I couldn't take part in physical activities. I had to figure out how to be part of the team without actually being part of the team, so instead I ran the scoreboard for basketball and attended every football and wrestling match I could to cheer on the teams to victory.

I found ways to be part of my community.

College life came in the fall of 2006 and I was quickly on my own. The community was no longer built in. I had to be willing to open myself up in ways I hadn't done before. For example, starting conversations, finding people to connect with, and being willing to ask for help from complete strangers are all things I had to learn to do."

The Wheel Truth

CHAPTER TEN

How to Build
a Support Community

All of us need people to be in our corner. Sometimes we need people beside us who understand our pain and sadness. When we have goals and desires for our life and we don't quite know how to reach them there are mentors, coaches, networking groups, and others who are willing to share their expertise. There are times of celebration and joy where we want to gather one and all to share in the moments of happiness. Whatever stage you're in, we ALL need growing communities of people we can depend on and those who can depend on us.

> **We've been sold this lie that disability makes you exceptional and it honestly doesn't...I want to live in a world where we don't have such low expectations of disabled people that we are congratulated for getting out of bed and remembering our own names in the morning.**
>
> *~ Stella Young*

For me, it's about wanting more for my life. I want more freedom, more independence, and more opportunities to reach the potential I know I'm capable of reaching. Many times, when you have a disability, you're told what your expectations should be for your life. I want to prove to people with and without disabilities that expectations can and should be defined by YOU first and foremost.

When I first knew I wanted and needed to begin a career in public speaking I had no idea where to start. However,

The Wheel Truth

I have a friend who speaks for a living, so I decided to sit down with him and discuss where to start. He suggested I join a Toastmasters organization to learn the bare bones of speaking. Once I became a member of Toastmasters, I gained not only the knowledge of speaking for a beginner, but I had mentors come alongside me who guided me closer to my end goal. After three years of being a Toastmasters member, I felt it was time to move on. I reconnected with a classmate from high school who introduced me to an entrepreneurship group called Impactful People. This is when real personal growth and connection with the "right" people started to happen. Through Impactful People, more opportunities came to connect with coaches and other business networking groups.

Support is essential to success when it comes to pursuing any goal or destroying any bad habit. Support groups are a good way to find the support you need from people whose struggle is similar to yours. These people can share ideas and advice or provide a listening ear for you to pour your heart out and voice your concerns with no judgment. It's important you find the group that fits your needs. www.gratitudelodge.com Search support groups

I've personally witnessed people with disabilities feeling lonely and depressed. Every disability is different with different levels of need. For me, it's been hard at times to find the "right" support. I'm part of a group called Wheel Connect, however. This group is made up of people with only physical disabilities. Through our connection we're able to feel empowered and take control of our lives. We also have conversations about the resources we all use and are able to give reliable feedback to one another. This group makes me feel like I have "disability" support, but our disabilities aren't the focal point of why we meet. www.mayoclinic.org Search healthy lifestyles

Here are some ways to increase your supportive community. If you want to get to know some of your neighbors maybe have a block or house party and invite them over. You could also watch out for each other by having a "neighborhood" watch team. These teams usually watch for crime, or any other unusual activity. If everyone is interested in this idea contact information can be exchanged.

Volunteering your time is also a great way to meet people. Personally, I've spoken on many disability panels and attended many disability events. While some of my political views aren't identical to many of my friends in the disability community, I still find it essential to be involved politically because almost everything discussed disability or not affects my quality of life. I developed a professional relationship with one of my local representatives and have kept in touch with him. This is why it's important for me to stay active in my community; I honestly never know who I'm going to connect with from day to day. https://www.wikihow.com/Get-Involved-in-Your-Community

When thinking about forming a community it's important to ask yourself these questions. What kind of support am I looking for? What kind of goals am I trying to accomplish? Am I willing to be pushed past my limits? Am I willing to be critiqued? These questions can sometimes be hard to answer honestly and to face, but if you desire true community these questions are necessary.

For me, it took a number of years to get my community to where it is today. I had to begin deciding what I wanted out of life. I had to figure out what MY goals were. I had to push past my limits (or what I thought my limitations were) and make the decision to want more. It hasn't always been easy, but it has been worth every drop of sweat as well as the many tears. A supportive community is what you make it to be.

Today I use these strategies and apply them in a whole new way while building my business. Don't get me wrong, it has been scary, but worth it in every possible way. I just continue to ask myself the questions I mentioned in the beginning: "Who am I? Where do I belong? and What are my values?" while also continuing to grow in the process.

CPSIA information can be obtained
at www.ICGtesting.com
Printed in the USA
BVHW021132160220
572463BV00003B/11

9 781792 326004